# Voyages to the New World

Peter Chrisp

Thomson Learning
New York

# Exploration & Encounters 1450-1550
## The Search for the East
## Voyages to the New World
## The Spanish Conquest of Central and South America
## The Search for a Northern Route

Cover pictures: Ptolemy's world map, recreated in 1486; and a nineteenth-century woodcut showing the discovery of the Strait of Magellan in 1520.
Title page picture: An eighteenth-century illustration of the preparations for Columbus's voyage of 1492.

First published in the United States in 1993 by
Thomson Learning
115 Fifth Avenue
New York, NY 10003

First published in 1993 by Wayland (Publishers) Ltd.

Cataloging-in-Publication Data applied for

ISBN: 1-56847-121-1

Printed in Italy

**Picture acknowledgments**
The publishers would like to thank the following for permission to use their pictures in this book: Ancient Art & Architecture Collection 33 (top); Archiv für Kunst und Geschichte main cover picture, title page, 5 (both), 6, 10, 12, 13, 14 (both), 15, 23, 24, 25, 26, 27 (both), 29 (bottom), 30, 31, 33 (bottom), 35, 36, 37 (top), 38, 39, 40 (bottom), 42, 44; Bridgeman Art Library 7 (both); E. T. Archives 19; Mary Evans 28, 40 (top), 41; Michael Holford cover (map), 4, 16; Mansell 29 (top), 32; Photri 8, 9, 43; Wayland Picture Library 18. The artwork was supplied by Mike Taylor.

## SOURCES OF QUOTES

Page 7: Ronald Latham (trans.), *The Travels of Marco Polo* (Penguin, 1958), p. 113 and p. 126 (1st quote), p. 244 (2d quote).
Page 9: Abu 'Abdullah al-Idrisi, *The Book of Roger*, quoted by Bjorn Landstrom, *The Quest for India* (Allen & Unwin, 1964), p. 85.
Page 10: Pierre d'Ailly, *The Image of the World*, quoted by Samuel Eliot Morison, *Admiral of the Ocean Sea. A Life of Christopher Columbus* (Little, Brown and Company, 1942), p. 123.
Page 13: João de Barros, *Decades of Asia* (1552), quoted by Samuel Eliot Morison, *op. cit.*, p. 94.
Page 18: Eugenio de Salazar, *Letter to the Licentiate Miranda de Ron*, 1573, in J. H. Parry, *The European Reconnaissance. Selected Documents* (Macmillan, 1968), pp. 356-7.
Page 21: The ships' boys' cry is also quoted by Salazar in his letter, p. 350 in the above source.
Page 23: Extracts from Columbus's log from John Cummins, *The Voyage of Christopher Columbus. Columbus's Own Journal of Discovery Newly Restored and Translated* (Weidenfeld & Nicolson, 1992), p. 88, p. 92.
Page 25: *Ibid*, p. 94.
Page 27: *Ibid*, p. 96.
Page 35: Amerigo Vespucci, letter to Lorenzo di Medici, March 1503, from C. R. Markham (ed.), *The Letters of Amerigo Vespucci* (Hakluyt Society, 1894), p. 42.
Page 37: Gonzalo de Oviedo, *General History of the Indies* (1534), extract in J.H. Parry, *op. cit.*, p. 234.
Page 39: Antonio Pigafetta in Charles E. Nowell (ed.), *Magellan's Voyage Around the World. Three Contemporary Accounts* (Northwestern University Press, 1962), pp. 101-2.
Page 41: *Ibid*, pp. 122-3.
Page 43: Juan del Cano, letter to Charles V, September 1522, quoted by Samuel Eliot Morison, *The European Discovery of America. The Southern Voyages 1492-1616* (Oxford University Press, 1974), p. 472.

# CONTENTS

# The World in 1492

For thousands of years, people knew very little about their world. Native Americans did not know that there were other lands – Europe, Asia, Australia and Africa – where other people lived. In the same way, Europeans had no idea that America existed.

Between 1492 and 1522, the Spanish sent out a series of

This map shows what Europeans thought the world looked like before their voyages of exploration.

voyagers across the seas, which brought the two worlds together for the first time. The sailors were looking for Asia, but landed in America. At first, they did not realize what they had found – they thought that America was part of Asia. When they realized that America was a continent, they were amazed. They began to call America a "new world."

This book is about a tiny period of human history – just thirty years. Yet this short period saw an incredible growth in human knowledge.

In 1492, Europeans did not know what lay across the Atlantic Ocean. Thirty years later, they had sailed all the way around the world.

*Above* Spanish explorers landing in the "new world," watched over by their king back in Europe. This woodcut was printed in 1493.

*Left* This world map, painted in 1571 and showing the American continent, was made possible by exploration.

# The Riches of the Indies

In the fifteenth century, Europeans had only vague ideas about the lands of Asia. They knew the names – India, Cathay (China), and Cipangu (Japan) – but they had no idea where these countries were in relation to each other. To Europeans, they were all part of the Indies, the lands that lay to the east.

Stories about these places sometimes reached Europe. Marco Polo, a merchant from Italy, had traveled overland to China in the thirteenth century. He had brought back stories of the Indies. According to Marco Polo, these were lands of unbelievable wealth. They were rich in gold, precious stones, and spices.

Marco Polo watches the people of the Indies collecting spices, which were rare and valuable goods in Europe.

Marco Polo spent many years at the court of Kublai Khan, the fabulously wealthy ruler of China. He wrote:

*The title Khan means "Great Lord of Lords." And certainly he has every right to this title; for everyone should know that this Great Khan is the mightiest man who has ever lived . . . His palace is so vast and so well built that no man in the world could think of any way to improve it. The roof is ablaze with scarlet and green and blue and yellow, so brilliantly varnished that it glitters like crystal.*

Polo did not visit Cipangu (Japan), but he heard tales in China of its wealth:

*They have gold in plenty . . . The ruler has a very large palace entirely roofed with fine gold. Just as we roof our houses or churches with lead, so this palace is roofed with fine gold.*

Kublai Khan (1216-1294).

Many Europeans thought that Marco Polo's stories were lies and exaggerations. But some people believed them and began to look for new ways to reach the wealth of the Indies.

The Indies were thought to be rich in precious stones.

# The Sea of Darkness

In 1300, the Atlantic Ocean was an unknown sea. No one knew how big it was, or whether it was possible to sail across it. Because it was unknown, people imagined it was full of terrors. They believed in sea monsters, such as giant serpents, which could gobble up a whole ship.

Most of the storms that hit the coasts of western Europe came from the direction of the Atlantic. So the sea also came to be known as a place of

A giant sea serpent snatches a sailor from his ship. Some early sailors believed that huge and terrifying sea monsters like this lived in the waters of the Atlantic Ocean.

storms. It was said to be a sea where ships would suddenly be lost in thick fogs. Only the bravest sailors had the courage to travel far across such a sea.

From the 1300s, European sailors began to venture away from the coastline and sail into this unknown sea. They found islands: the Canaries, Madeira, and the Azores. An important advance was that sailors had begun to understand the Atlantic wind system. Learning which way the winds blew was the first step to sailing successfully across the Atlantic and back.

No one knew what frightening things lay in wait for ships that ventured away from the coastline and into the unknown seas.

The Muslims called the Atlantic the "green sea of darkness." In the twelfth century, a Muslim mapmaker called Abu 'Abdullah al-Idrisi, who served King Roger II of Sicily, wrote:

*No seafarer dares to sail out into the Atlantic Sea and steer a course away from land. Men sail along the coastline and never leave it out of sight . . . What lies beyond the sea is known to no man. No one has yet been able to discover anything that is to be trusted with regard to this ocean, because of the difficulties in the way of seafaring, the lack of light, and the many storms.*

# Christopher Columbus

Christopher Columbus was born in 1451 in Genoa, a seaport in northern Italy. At an early age he went to sea, sailing on trading ships in the Mediterranean. In the 1470s, Columbus moved to Portugal. From there he made several voyages in the Atlantic Ocean.

Although this portrait was painted after Columbus's death, it matches written descriptions of him.

Columbus read many geography books to find support for his idea. His favorite book was *The Image of the World* written by Cardinal Pierre d'Ailly in 1410. In this book, d'Ailly wrote: ***Between the end of Spain and the beginning of India lies a narrow sea that can be sailed in a few days with a favorable wind.***

Like all educated Europeans, Columbus believed that the Indies could be reached by sailing west, across the Atlantic. The question was, how far away were the Indies? Columbus thought they were only 2,400 miles away.

His incorrect calculations were based on the mistaken but widely believed idea

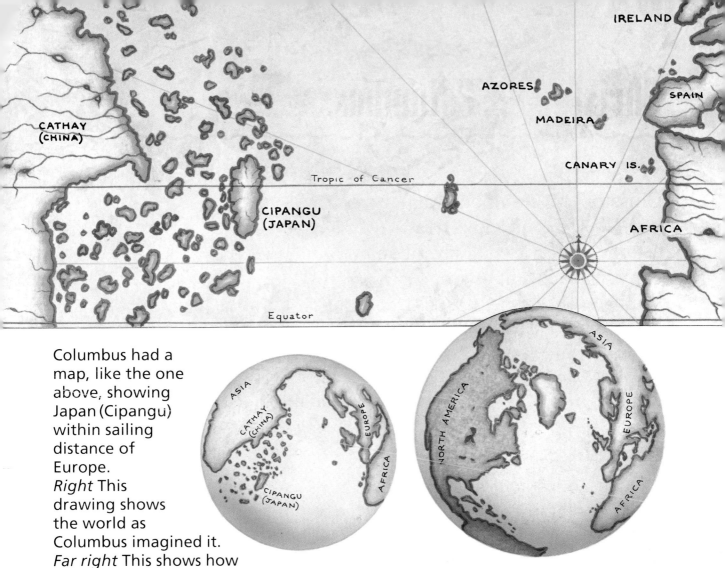

IRELAND

AZORES

SPAIN

MADEIRA

CATHAY
(CHINA)

CANARY IS.

Tropic of Cancer

CIPANGU
(JAPAN)

AFRICA

Equator

Columbus had a map, like the one above, showing Japan (Cipangu) within sailing distance of Europe.
*Right* This drawing shows the world as Columbus imagined it.
*Far right* This shows how much bigger the world really is, with America between Europe and Japan.

ASIA

CATHAY
(CHINA)

EUROPE

AFRICA

CIPANGU
(JAPAN)

ASIA

NORTH AMERICA

EUROPE

AFRICA

that six-sevenths of the earth was dry land. This dry land could only be Europe, Africa, and Asia, Columbus reasoned, so these lands must cover most of the earth. This led Columbus to believe that the world was much smaller than it really is.

Columbus decided that he was the man to sail across the Atlantic and find Asia. He wanted to become rich and famous. But he was also very religious. He believed that he had been given a special task by God – to take Christianity to the Indies.

11

# Columbus's Search For a Sponsor

Before he could sail, Columbus needed to find a sponsor – someone who would pay for a voyage across the Atlantic. Voyages of exploration were expensive and risky. Many explorers disappeared. Others returned without finding anything useful. The ships, equipment, and the wages of the crews all cost money.

The likeliest people to sponsor an expedition were the rulers of Europe. They were the ones with the most money, and they would have the most to gain from the discovery of unknown lands. But no ruler would pay for a voyage of exploration simply on the chance that it *might* find new lands. Columbus had to convince them that he had a very good chance of succeeding.

Columbus waits at the royal court of Spain, while experts look at his plans. A world map lies at Columbus's feet.

In 1484, Columbus went to King John of Portugal to ask for his backing. King John's experts looked at the plan for a year before they decided to reject it. The Portuguese were putting all their efforts into finding a southeastern route to the Indies, sailing around Africa. They had no money to spare for Columbus.

Queen Isabella of Spain, who agreed to sponsor Columbus.

 João de Barros, a Portuguese writer, described what happened when Columbus took his plan to King John of Portugal:

**The king, seeing this Christovao Colom to be a big talker and boastful and very full of fantasy and imagination, had little faith in him . . . [The king's advisers] considered the words of Christovao Colom as empty, simply based on imagination like that same island Cipangu of Marco Polo.**

Next, Columbus went to King Ferdinand and Queen Isabella of Spain. The queen was impressed by Columbus; like him, she was very religious. But in the 1480s, the Spanish were busy fighting a war against the Muslims who still ruled part of Spain. It wasn't until this war was won, in 1492, that Ferdinand and Isabella agreed to pay for Columbus's voyage.

# Ships for the Voyage

In May 1492, Columbus went to the port of Palos on Spain's southwestern coast to prepare three ships for the voyage. The ships were all trading vessels, called caravels. Two were light, fast ships. Their names were the *Niña* and the *Pinta*. The third, the *Santa María*, was a larger, heavier, and slower type of ship. This was to be Columbus's flagship.

*Right* The Pinzón brothers: Vicente (top), captain of the *Niña*, and Martin (bottom), captain of the *Pinta*. Vicente, the younger brother, is pictured holding a quadrant.

In Palos, Columbus was lucky to get the help of the Pinzón brothers, Martin and Vicente. They belonged to an important local seafaring family. The brothers offered to captain the two smaller caravels, and they set about recruiting sailors to man the ships. This was not an easy task. Columbus was an unknown foreigner in Palos. His plans were thought to be risky and uncertain. Without the Pinzón brothers he would have had trouble getting people to volunteer for such a voyage.

It took ten weeks to get the ships ready and to hire ninety men and boys for the voyage. The ships were loaded with enough food to last a year, as well as tools, weapons, and other equipment.

On August 3, 1492, the little fleet at last set sail from the port of Palos.

Columbus says goodbye to King Ferdinand and Queen Isabella and goes to join his ships, waiting in the harbor of Palos.

Here is a list of some of the things that the three ships carried:

Planks of wood, nails, sailcloth, ropes, tar, anchors.

Guns, crossbows, swords, ammunition, armor.

Casks of water and wine, flour, olive oil, ship's biscuit (hard, flat baked bread), beans, peas, and salted meat and fish.

Cooking pots and bowls.

Fishing nets and hooks.

Compasses, spare compass needles, quadrants, and charts for navigation.

Glass beads, brass bells, and knitted caps for trading.

Small samples of gold and spices.

A letter from King Ferdinand and Queen Isabella to give to the Great Khan of China.

# Navigation

The most important men on each ship were the navigators, the people whose job was to find the way at sea. As well as a captain, each ship had a master and a pilot, who were second and third in command. All of them helped to navigate the ship.

The most important instrument on board ship was the compass, a device with a magnetic needle that always points north.

The main method of navigation was "dead reckoning." This meant working out the speed of the ship and the direction it was traveling (using a compass), and then marking the ship's course on a chart. This took great skill. The navigator had to take account of changing winds and currents that might send his ship off course.

Columbus also had an instrument called a quadrant. He could use this on clear nights to measure the height of the North Star. Its position could show him how far to the north or south he was.

The sailors dropped lines weighted with lead over the side of the ship to test the depth of the water. This told them whether the seabed was sloping up toward a coast.

Practical experience was as important as instruments. Good navigators could judge the depth of the water by its color. They would watch the sky for birds and the sea for floating twigs. Both might be signs of land.

Tools for Navigation

LEAD AND LINE: THE SAILOR HELD A LINE WEIGHTED WITH LEAD OVER THE SIDE OF THE SHIP TO MEASURE THE DEPTH OF THE WATER.

TRAVERSE BOARD: THIS WAS USED TOGETHER WITH A COMPASS AND SAND-GLASS. EVERY HALF-HOUR THE PEGS WERE MOVED TO SHOW THE DIRECTION AND DISTANCE TRAVELLED BY THE SHIP.

QUADRANT: THE NAVIGATOR POINTED THE STRAIGHT EDGE AT THE POLE STAR OR MIDDAY SUN TO MEASURE ITS HEIGHT IN THE SKY. THIS WOULD TELL HIM HOW FAR TO THE NORTH OR SOUTH HE WAS.

# Life at Sea

Columbus's tiny ships must have been very uncomfortable. There were no special sleeping quarters, so the sailors often slept out on the open deck. There were no toilets either. The men had to relieve themselves over the sides – even in rough weather.

It was difficult to keep clean. The sailors only had sea water in which to wash, and they would let their beards grow.

Many years later, a Spaniard called Eugenio de Salazar described life at sea in a letter:

*The worst longing is for something to drink. You are in the middle of the sea, surrounded by water, but they dole out the water by ounces, and all the time you are dying of thirst from eating dried beef and food pickled in brine . . . Even the water, when you can get it, is so foul that you have to close your eyes and hold your nose before you can swallow it . . . The people around you will belch, or vomit, or break wind, or empty their bowels, while you are having your breakfast.*

Cramped life aboard a ship of Columbus's time. One sailor is vomiting over the side.

This seventeenth-century painting shows the *Santa María* at the start of the voyage.

They lived and slept in the same clothes, and it is not surprising that they became infested with lice and fleas.

If the sailors were lucky, they were given one hot meal a day. This was cooked on a fire box (a tray filled with sand) on which the ship's boys built a fire. The boys cooked meat or fish in olive oil, and baked bread in the ashes. Because the fire box was on the deck, they could not build a fire when it was raining. They had to make do with eating dry ship's biscuit.

Cooped up together on a small ship, with only the wide, flat sea surrounding them, the sailors would become foul tempered and bored.

# The Sailors' Day

The crew of each ship was divided into two "watches." Each watch ran the ship for four hours, while sailors from the other watch rested. The youngest boy kept track of the time with the sandglass. Every half-hour the sand would run out and he would turn the glass over, shouting out the hour. The lookouts, one in the bow and one perched high on the mainmast, would shout back to prove that they were awake.

The officer in charge watched the sails and the sea for changes in the wind. Then he would shout orders to the helmsman, who steered the ship, and to the sailors to hoist or lower sails. They sang a special chant as they hauled at the ropes that raised the heavy sails.

When they were not handling the sails, the men were kept busy scrubbing the decks with sea water and making repairs. Each morning, they pumped out the water that had leaked into the ship's hold.

Religion was very important to all the sailors. They knew that they were at the mercy of the sea and the winds, and they prayed for good weather. Throughout the day, the youngest boys on each ship led the crews in prayers. At nightfall, each crew joined together to sing "Salve Regina," a hymn to the Virgin Mary.

Each morning, the ships' boys would cry out these words: ***Blessed be the light of day, and the Holy True Cross . . . May God give us a fair day and a good voyage. May the ship make a swift passage, with her captain, master, and fine ship's company.***

**The Santa María**
The inside of Columbus's ship probably looked like this.

MAINMAST

FIRE BOX

PUMPS

SHIP'S HOLD

Ship's equipment

# Across the Atlantic

After leaving Spain, the ships headed southwest, toward the Canary Islands. Columbus believed that if he sailed west from the Canaries he would reach Cipangu (Japan). He also knew that the winds in the Canaries usually blew to the west. They would help him on his way. If he had sailed west from Spain, he would have had to battle against the wind.

After a stop for repairs in the Canaries, the ships headed off across the unknown ocean. The winds were perfect and the ships made good speed.

As the days passed without sight of land, the sailors grew more and more troubled.

This map shows Columbus's voyage across the Atlantic in 1492 and his return to Spain in 1493.

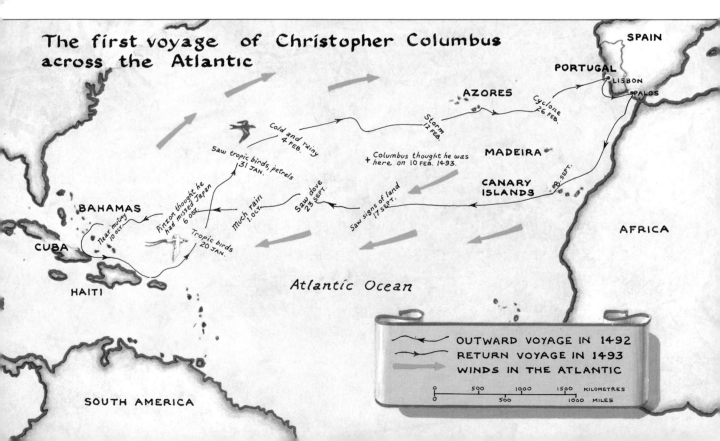

The first voyage of Christopher Columbus across the Atlantic

SPAIN
PORTUGAL
LISBON
PALOS
AZORES
Cyclone 26 FEB.
Storm 12 FEB.
Cold and rainy 4 FEB.
Columbus thought he was here on 10 FEB. 1493.
MADEIRA
Saw tropic birds, petrels 31 JAN.
CANARY ISLANDS
8 SEPT.
Pinzon thought he had missed Japan 6 OCT.
Much rain 1 OCT.
Saw dove 23 SEPT.
Saw signs of land 17 SEPT.
BAHAMAS
Near mutiny 10 OCT.
Tropic birds 20 JAN.
AFRICA
CUBA
HAITI
Atlantic Ocean
SOUTH AMERICA

OUTWARD VOYAGE IN 1492
RETURN VOYAGE IN 1493
WINDS IN THE ATLANTIC
0   500   1000   1500   KILOMETRES
0      500      1000   MILES

Extracts from Columbus's log:

*I have been going around encouraging the men . . . The further we sail from Spain the greater grows their distress and unrest; they complain more every hour.*      September 19

*They could contain themselves no longer and began to complain of the length of the voyage. I encouraged them as best as I could, trying to raise their hopes of the benefits they might gain from it. I also told them that it was useless to complain. Having set out for the Indies I shall continue this voyage until, with God's grace, I reach them.*      October 10

A nineteenth-century painting of unrest among the sailors on the *Santa María*. In fact, none of Columbus's men threatened him with weapons.

None of them had been at sea for such a long time. They worried because the winds that pushed them onward were so strong – would they ever find a wind blowing east to take them home again? Sometimes their hopes were falsely raised – a low cloud on the horizon would be mistaken for land.

Columbus's main concern was keeping the crew happy. There was always a risk that they might mutiny, refusing to obey his orders and forcing him to turn back.

# "Land! Land!"

In the early morning of October 12, the cry that everyone had been waiting for came from the lookout on the *Pinta*: "Land! Land!" After a month at sea, a small, low-lying island had been sighted.

At daybreak, the three ships sailed into a lagoon and dropped anchor. The sailors could see groups of naked, brown-skinned people watching them from the shore. These people must have been astonished at the wooden ships, larger than any they had known, and at the pale-skinned men who wore clothes. But they gave the strangers a friendly welcome.

Columbus went ashore in a small boat bristling with weapons. Watched by the curious people on the beach,

A sixteenth-century picture shows Columbus sighting land. His ship is surrounded by images of ancient gods of the sea.

24

Columbus lands and is greeted by the Taino. His men set up a cross as a sign that they have brought a new religion to the island. Not surprisingly, some of the Tainos are shown running away – what could they have thought when they saw these ships?

he unfurled the royal flag and proclaimed that the new land belonged to the King and Queen of Spain.

The people watching Columbus called themselves the Taino, a word meaning "good people," and they called their island Guanahani. However, Columbus was convinced that he had reached the Indies and so he called them Indians. He called the island San Salvador. Today it is also known as Watling Island. It is in the Bahamas.

In his log, Columbus described the people he had found:

*They do not carry weapons or know of them, for I showed them swords and they took them by the blade and cut themselves through ignorance . . . They should be good and clever servants, since I saw that they quickly took in what was said to them. I believe they would easily be made Christians, as it seemed to me they had no religion.*

# The Taino

The Taino of Guanahani were just one of the many peoples who lived on the islands. They were part of a larger group of peoples called the Arawak. The Taino painted themselves in patterns of red, white, and black. They lived in houses made from palm branches and slept in nets slung from posts, which they called *hamacas* (we now call them hammocks). They carved tree trunks into fishing boats called *canoas*.

Columbus was wrong to say that the Taino had no religion. They believed in a great god who lived in the sky, as well as many different spirits called *zemis*. They kept clay figures of these *zemis* in their houses and offered food and drink to them.

The Taino had no idea that Columbus's ships came from distant lands across an ocean.

The Taino lived in thatched houses built from palm trees.

On October 14, Columbus wrote in his log:

*We understood them to be asking if we had come from the sky. One old man climbed into the boat, and the others, men and women, kept shouting, "Come and see the men who have come from the sky! Bring them food and drink!"*

They did not know that distant lands existed. So they came to the conclusion that the strangers had come from the sky.

Many things about the strange visitors must have baffled the Taino, especially their obsession with gold. In the islands, copper was much more highly valued than gold. Useful tools could be made with copper, but gold was only good for ornaments.

The Taino decorated their bodies with painted patterns and may have looked something like this South American woman.

An early sixteenth-century woodcut of the Carib or Caniba people who lived to the southeast of the Taino. The Caribs were thought to eat human flesh.

# Columbus in the Islands

Columbus wanted to press on to find Cipangu and then the mainland. He was sure that these lands, with their cities and heaps of gold, must be very close.

The ships sailed south, stopping at a string of small islands and looking for people with gold. The Taino he met told him, through signs, that there was a large island to the southwest. Columbus hoped that this would be Cipangu at last.

On October 28, Columbus reached this large island, which the local people called Cuba. He sent some of his men inland to find the king. They found a large village where they were welcomed. The Spaniards tried out new foods, like maize and sweet potatoes. They saw people smoking the leaves of a strange plant,

The first sight of a Taino smoking tobacco must have been very strange to the Spaniards. There was nothing like it in Europe.

tobacco. But they found no gold and no cities.

Leaving Cuba, Columbus sailed southeast and found another large island. He was amazed at its beauty and lush green trees. It seemed to have more people than Cuba, and some of them wore gold nose ornaments. Columbus called the island Hispaniola, or "the Spanish Island."

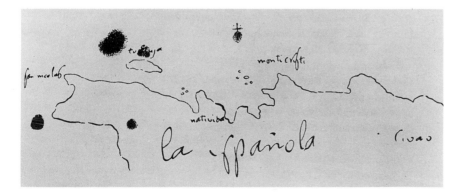

*Above* Columbus's flagship, the *Santa María*, was wrecked on a reef.
*Left* This is Columbus's own sketch of the coast of Hispaniola. He gave Spanish names to different areas.

The Spaniards stayed for several weeks, giving the Indians small bells in return for tiny amounts of gold. Then the *Santa María* was wrecked on a reef. Columbus decided to set sail home to Spain, leaving 39 of his men behind to look for gold and learn more about the island.

# Return to Spain

Columbus caused a sensation when he returned to the Spanish court. He had brought back six "Indians." On the voyage, they had been taught to sing the hymn "Hail Mary." They sang this for the king and queen. Then the rulers were shown cages

Columbus's triumphant return to the king and queen of Spain.

holding colorful parrots. Finally, Columbus brought out some gold – he had not found much, but he told the court that it was just a small sample of the great wealth of the islands.

Ferdinand and Isabella were delighted. Now they had the chance to spread their religion to new lands and to make Spain rich and powerful at the same time. The whole court knelt, thanking God.

Columbus was made a nobleman and richly rewarded. He was invited to ride by the king's side – something that only members of the royal family had been allowed to do. From then on, he would be known as the Admiral of the Ocean Sea. It was his moment of triumph.

In September 1493, Columbus sailed back to Hispaniola with a fleet of seventeen ships. This time, the aim was to make a Spanish settlement on the island – to build a town, plant crops, and mine for gold. The settlement could then be the base for more voyages of exploration to the mainland of China.

This 1493 woodcut shows the islands visited by Columbus. He gave them Spanish names and called two of them after Ferdinand and Isabella.

# The Spanish Settlers

Sailing in Columbus's second fleet were almost 1,500 men. There were soldiers, farmers, government officials, gentlemen in search of gold

Columbus's sailors had built a fort on Hispaniola for the men who were left behind on the first voyage. They used parts from the wrecked *Santa Maria.*

and adventure, and priests whose job would be to convert the local people to Christianity. All of them hoped to make a new life in the Indies. They brought tools, seeds from more than 100 plants, and farm animals.

Columbus's three tiny ships had amazed the Taino. Imagine the effect that this large fleet must have had! The Spaniards brought many animals the Taino had never seen. There were horses, cattle, sheep, goats, donkeys, pigs, dogs, cats, and chickens.

Columbus expected to find the men he had left behind on his first voyage. By now, he thought, these Spaniards would all have vast amounts of gold. He was shocked to learn that all of them had been killed by the local people.

The Spanish settlers hated life on Hispaniola. It always seemed to be raining and they began to suffer from strange new sicknesses. Many of the seeds they brought would not grow in the climate, and they ran short of food.

The Taino were forced to work for the Spaniards, to provide them with gold and food. But there was not much gold on Hispaniola. The Taino could not satisfy the demands of the angry Spaniards. Soon, there was open warfare. The Taino were no match for European weapons. They were killed in vast numbers or captured and made into slaves.

*Above* The Spaniards forced the local people to find gold for them. This picture shows Indians panning a river-bed – trying to sift out any gold that might have been washed into the river from inland.

*Below* Spaniards attack a village. The local people were helpless against the steel swords and guns of the Europeans.

# A New World?

Columbus made two more voyages of exploration, in 1498 and 1502. On the first of them, he found the mouth of a wide river, the Orinoco. Such a river could only come from a large area of land, a continent or mainland rather than an island.

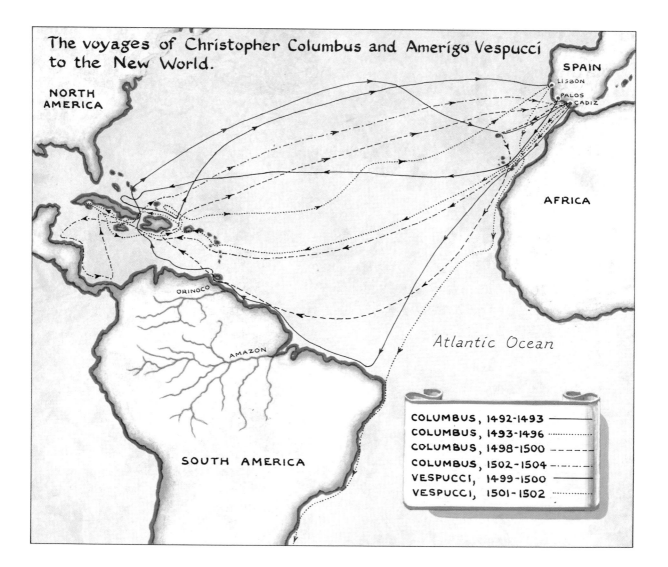

The voyages of Christopher Columbus and Amerigo Vespucci to the New World.

NORTH AMERICA

SPAIN
LISBON
PALOS
CADIZ

AFRICA

ORINOCO

AMAZON

Atlantic Ocean

SOUTH AMERICA

COLUMBUS, 1492-1493
COLUMBUS, 1493-1496
COLUMBUS, 1498-1500
COLUMBUS, 1502-1504
VESPUCCI, 1499-1500
VESPUCCI, 1501-1502

In 1503, Amerigo Vespucci wrote about the new world:

*It is lawful to call it a new world, because none of these countries were known to our ancestors, and to all who hear about them they will be entirely new . . .*
*I have found a continent, more full of people and animals than our Europe or Asia or Africa.*

Of course, this new world was only new to the people of Europe. For the millions of people who already lived there, it was a very old world.

Amerigo Vespucci. Unlike Columbus, Vespucci realized that the "new world" was not part of Asia. The "new" land of America was named after him.

Columbus described it as a "new world." Yet he still believed that this "new world" was part of the Indies. In fact, he was on the northeastern coast of South America.

Soon, the seas around the newly discovered lands were full of Spanish, then Portuguese and English ships. They explored the mainland to the south and north and began to realize it was not part of Asia.

In 1507, German mapmaker Martin Waldseemüller suggested that the new land be called America after an Italian explorer Amerigo Vespucci, who had made voyages to the mainland in 1499 and 1501. Vespucci's account of the new world had been read all over Europe. He claimed all credit for the discovery of America himself.

# Balboa finds the Pacific

America was not part of Asia. Rather, it was a barrier. Asia lay still farther to the west, across another large body of water – later to be called the Pacific Ocean.

Balboa traveled through swamps and jungle like this, depending on the local people to show him the way.

The first European to see the Pacific was a tough, redheaded Spanish adventurer called Vasco Núñez de Balboa. He had made himself leader of a Spanish settlement at Darien on the American mainland. In Darien, Balboa heard from the local people, the Cuna, that another sea lay a short distance away. Balboa took 190 Spaniards and 800 Cuna porters and set off to find it. For three weeks, they hacked their way through thick jungle and waded through swamps.

At last, on September 25, 1513, Balboa climbed a hill and saw the blue waters of the sea glittering in the distance. The Spaniards fell on their knees and gave thanks to God for letting them find this sea. Balboa had crossed America at its narrowest part, known today as Panama.

Vasco Nuñez toma posesion de laMar
del Sur

*Left* Waving his sword, Balboa wades into the Pacific, shouting out that this vast sea now "belongs" to Spain.

*Below* This map shows Balboa's route from the Spanish settlement, Santa Maria, along the coast by sea and then across the land.

Gonzala Fernandez de Oviedo described how Balboa proclaimed the new sea belonged to Spain:

**With his drawn sword in his hand and his shield on his arm, he waded into the salt sea up to his knees, and paced back and forth reciting, 'For the royal crown of Castile [Spain], I now take possession of these southern seas, lands, coasts, harbors, and islands . . . And if any other prince should claim any right to these lands or seas, I am ready and armed to defy him . . .'"**

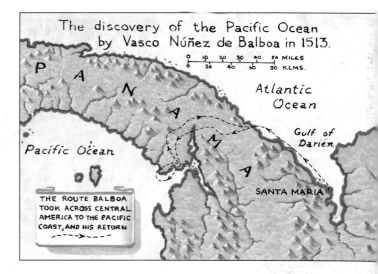

The discovery of the Pacific Ocean by Vasco Núñez de Balboa in 1513.

P A N A M A

Atlantic Ocean

Pacific Ocean

Gulf of Darien

SANTA MARIA

THE ROUTE BALBOA TOOK ACROSS CENTRAL AMERICA TO THE PACIFIC COAST, AND HIS RETURN
- - - ->

His discovery raised hopes that there might be a sea passage through the continent. If one could be found, Asia might still be only a short distance away. Columbus's scheme of sailing west to the Indies might still work.

# Magellan's Search for a Strait

While the Spanish were exploring the new world to the west, the Portuguese had found a route to Asia by sailing east. This route, around Africa, was very slow. Ships were lost in storms off southern Africa and many sailors died on the long voyage.

Ferdinand Magellan was a Portuguese nobleman who had served his country as a soldier in the Indies. Like Columbus, he believed that a western voyage would be much quicker than the Portuguese route. He was sure there was a strait, or sea passage, through the American continent, and that Asia was close beyond.

Magellan was turned down by his own king, but Charles I, the new king of Spain, agreed to sponsor the plan. He gave Magellan five small ships and about 265 men.

Ferdinand Magellan led perhaps the greatest of all voyages of exploration.

In September 1519, the ships set sail. For months, they traveled down the coast of America, looking for the strait. Magellan had to put down a mutiny. Then one of his ships was wrecked. It grew bitterly cold, and the sailors were forced to spend the winter on the coast of South America. A second ship then deserted and sailed back to Spain.

Magellan is seen here sailing through the Strait of Magellan into the wide waters of the Pacific Ocean, guided by ancient gods.

Yet Magellan did find a strait, today called the Strait of Magellan. It was much farther south than he had expected, and it took him thirty-eight days to find the way through. But it would all be worthwhile if the Indies lay close at hand.

Magellan named the southernmost part of America Patagonia (which means "big foot land"), after the tall people living there. Antonio Pigafetta, an Italian who sailed with Magellan, described meeting one of these giants: *One day, without anyone expecting it, we saw a giant, who was on the shore and who was dancing and leaping and singing . . . Our captain sent one of his men toward him, whom he ordered to sing and leap like the other to show him friendship . . . The captain caused food and drink to be given to this giant, then they showed him some things, including a mirror. When the giant saw his reflection in it, he was greatly terrified, leaping backwards and knocking over three or four of our men.*

# Across the Vast Pacific

Magellan named the newly found sea the Pacific, the peaceful sea. His ships sailed north and then west. He expected to reach the Indies within a few weeks. But what Magellan did not know is that the Pacific is the world's largest ocean. It covers more than a third of the earth's surface.

*Above* Only three ships out of Magellan's original fleet of five reached the Pacific Ocean.

*Left* Magellan (bottom left) takes his place with the heroes of Spanish exploration around this sixteenth-century map of America. Columbus is top left and Vespucci top right. The fourth figure is Francisco Pizarro, conqueror of Peru.

Magellan sometimes had to punish his Spanish officers, who did not like being commanded by a foreigner.

There are islands in the Pacific but, unluckily, Magellan chose a course that made him miss most of them. The ships spent nearly four months in the open sea.

As the weeks turned into months, food supplies ran low. The men began to suffer from starvation and scurvy, a disease caused by lack of vitamin C, found in fresh vegetables and fruit.

Pigafetta, sailing with Magellan, described the terrible sufferings of the sailors on the ocean-crossing in his diary:

*For three months and twenty days, we could not take on board fresh supplies of food and drink. We ate only old ship's biscuit which turned to powder. It was swarming with maggots and stank of the urine of the rats that had eaten all the good biscuit. We drank water that was yellow and stinking. We also ate the leather which covered the main yard . . . We had to soak it in the sea for four or five days and then cook it on the hot cinders of a dying fire. Often we ate sawdust. Rats were sold for half a ducat [a gold coin], and even then we could not always get them. But above all the other misfortunes, the following was the worst. The gums of some of our men swelled, so that they could not eat and therefore died.*

# Return of the Survivors

In April 1521, Magellan's ships finally reached the Philippine Islands. But the sufferings of the explorer and his sailors were not over. Magellan offered to help the ruler of one island in a local war, and he was cut down with seven of his men in a battle. Then, twenty-eight sailors were murdered by the same ruler, after being invited to a feast.

There were now too few sailors to man the three remaining ships. One ship had to be abandoned. A second was captured by the Portuguese, who thought that only they had the right to sail in those waters. Most of its crew died as prisoners.

The remaining ship, the *Victoria*, commanded by Juan Sebastion del Cano, now sailed

*Left* The *Victoria* was the only ship of the original fleet to get back home to Spain. The ship carried a cargo of cloves which paid back the costs of the whole expedition.

*Right* This map of 1547 shows the route taken by the *Victoria*, the first ship to sail around the world.

slowly home, traveling west around Africa. On September 6, 1522, after many hardships, the *Victoria* struggled into a Spanish port. There were only seventeen other sailors on board, all sick with scurvy. They had been at sea for three years and they had sailed all the way around the world.

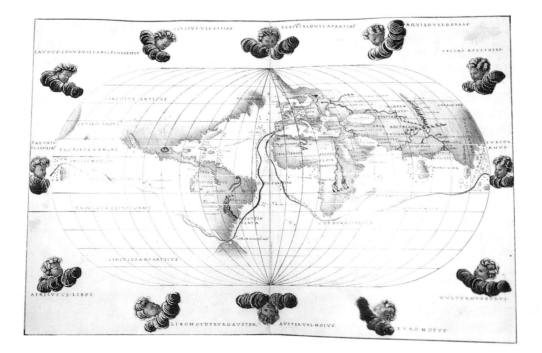 Juan del Cano described the last part of his voyage on the *Victoria* in his report to King Charles I: *In five months, we touched at no land for fear of the King of Portugal, who had given orders in all his lands to capture us . . . but we decided to die before falling into the hands of the Portuguese. And so with very great labor at the pumps, which we had to work night and day to free the ship of water, and as exhausted as any man ever was, with the help of God, and after a voyage of three years, we have arrived.*

# The Old World and the New

Magellan's voyage showed that it was possible to reach the Indies by sailing west. But you had to sail around a vast continent and then across the world's biggest ocean to get there. This was bad news for Spain. It meant that Portugal had found the quickest route to the Indies. Yet, although the Spanish had not found their shortcut, they had found something else – a new world called America.

This blue mask, decorated with turquoise and shell, was made by the Aztecs.

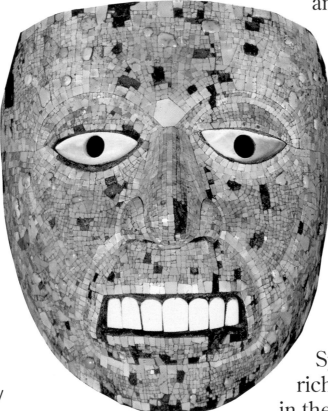

In 1519, a Spanish expedition from Cuba, led by Hernán Cortés, reached the coast of Mexico in Central America. The people there told Cortés of a great inland empire, ruled by a people called the Aztecs. It seemed that here at last were the cities and heaps of gold that Columbus had been looking for nearly thirty years before. The Spanish conquest of the American mainland had begun. It would make Spain the richest country in the world.

For the "Indians," as they were still called, the coming of the Europeans was a disaster that changed their lives forever. Tens of millions died from diseases, new to their lands, which were brought by the Europeans. Thousands more were worked to death in silver and gold mines and sugar plantations. Their old ways of life were destroyed.

By 1510, the Taino were dying so quickly that the Spaniards had to ship slaves from Africa to work on Hispaniola. Today, there are no Taino left on any of the islands Columbus's tiny fleet visited in 1492. They are an extinct people.

The voyages of exploration changed life in both the old and the new worlds. Here are a few of the things that passed from one to the other:

| From America to Europe | From Europe to America |
|---|---|
| Potatoes | Cattle |
| Tomatoes | Horses |
| Maize | Sheep |
| Kidney beans | Pigs |
| Chili peppers | Wheat |
| Peanuts | Sugarcane |
| Turkeys | Iron and steel |
| Chocolate | Wheeled transport |
| Tobacco | Christianity |
| Rubber | Diseases (smallpox, influenza, measles, chicken pox, typhus) |

45

# GLOSSARY

**Caravel** A light, fast trading ship used in many of the early voyages of exploration.

**Cathay** An old European name for China.

**Cipangu** An old European name for Japan.

**Compass** An instrument for finding direction. It uses a magnetic needle that always points north.

**Dead reckoning** A way of working out a ship's position by recording and comparing its speed and direction.

**Exploration** The search for unknown lands or new routes to known lands.

**Flagship** The ship that carries the commander of the fleet.

**Hold** The part of a ship, below deck, where cargo is stored.

**Log** A book in which all the details of a ship's voyage are recorded.

**Navigation** The science of finding the way from one place to another.

**Quadrant** An instrument for finding position to the north or south by measuring the height of the North Star or midday sun. The first quadrants were shaped like a quarter of a circle with a scale marked on the curved edge. A weighted line hung down from the corner. The navigator would point the straight edge at the star or sun, and then note the position on the scale touched by the line.

**Sandglass** An instrument for measuring a period of time, such as one half-hour. It is a glass container that is very thin in the middle. When it is turned upside down the sand inside will take one half-hour to fall from the top to the bottom.

**Scurvy** A disease caused by lack of vitamin C, once common on long voyages when supplies of fresh food, especially fruit, ran out.

**Serpent** An old word for snake.

**Ship's biscuit** Hard, flat, baked bread that was taken on long voyages, because it could be kept for a long time without going bad.

**Spices** The seeds, leaves, or bark of certain plants that grow in hot climates and give flavor to food, such as pepper, cinnamon, and nutmeg.

**Sponsor** A rich person, such as a king or queen, who provides money to put a plan into action.

**Strait** A narrow passage of water through land that joins two large areas of water or seas.

**Sweet potato** A plant with sweet, thick roots that can be eaten like potatoes. The plant comes from the West Indies and Central America.

**Taino** An extinct people who used to live on islands in the Caribbean, especially Cuba, Hispaniola, and the Bahamas.

**Yard** A beam holding the sail on the mast of a ship.

# BOOKS TO READ

Ash, Maureen. *Vasco Núñez de Balboa: Expedition to the Pacific Ocean.* The World's Great Explorers. Chicago: Childrens Press, 1990.

Asimov, Isaac. *Isaac Asimov's Pioneers of Science and Exploration.* 3 vols. Milwaukee: Gareth Stevens, 1991.

Grant, Neil. *The Great Atlas of Discovery.* New York: Knopf Books for Young Readers, 1992.

Humble, Richard. *The Age of Leif Erikson.* Exploration Through the Ages. New York: Franklin Watts, 1989.

Humble, Richard. *The Voyages of Columbus.* Exploration Through the Ages. New York: Franklin Watts, 1991.

Hunter, Nigel. *The Expeditions of Cortes.* Great Journeys. New York: Bookwright, 1990.

# INDEX